T0004832

# A PLACE FOR
# BATS

For Caroline Grace
*—M. S.*

For Patrycja Bond with gratitude
*—H. B.*

Published by
PEACHTREE PUBLISHING COMPANY INC.
1700 Chattahoochee Avenue
Atlanta, Georgia 30318-2112
*PeachtreeBooks.com*

Text © 2012, 2017 by Melissa Stewart
Illustrations © 2012, 2017 by Higgins Bond

All rights reserved. No part of this publication may be reproduced, stored in a retrieval system, or transmitted in any form or by any means—electronic, mechanical, photocopy, recording, or any other—except for brief quotations in printed reviews, without the prior permission of the publisher.

Book design by Loraine M. Joyner
Composition by Melanie McMahon Ives
Edited by Vicky Holifield

Illustrations created in acrylic on cold press illustration board.
Title typeset in Hardlyworthit; main text typeset in Monotype's Century Schoolbook with Optima initial capitals. Sidebars typeset in Optima.

Printed in June 2023 by Toppan Leefung in China

10 9 8 7 6 5 4 3 2 1 (hardcover)
20 19 18 17 16 15 (trade paperback)
Revised Edition

HC: 978-1-56145-762-5
PB: 978-1-56145-763-2

**Library of Congress Cataloging-in-Publication Data**
Stewart, Melissa.
A place for bats / written by Melissa Stewart ; illustrated by Higgins Bond.
p. cm.
ISBN 978-1-56145-624-6
1.  Bats—Juvenile literature.  I. Bond, Higgins, ill. II. Title.
QL737.C5S7447 2012
599.4—dc23
2011020468

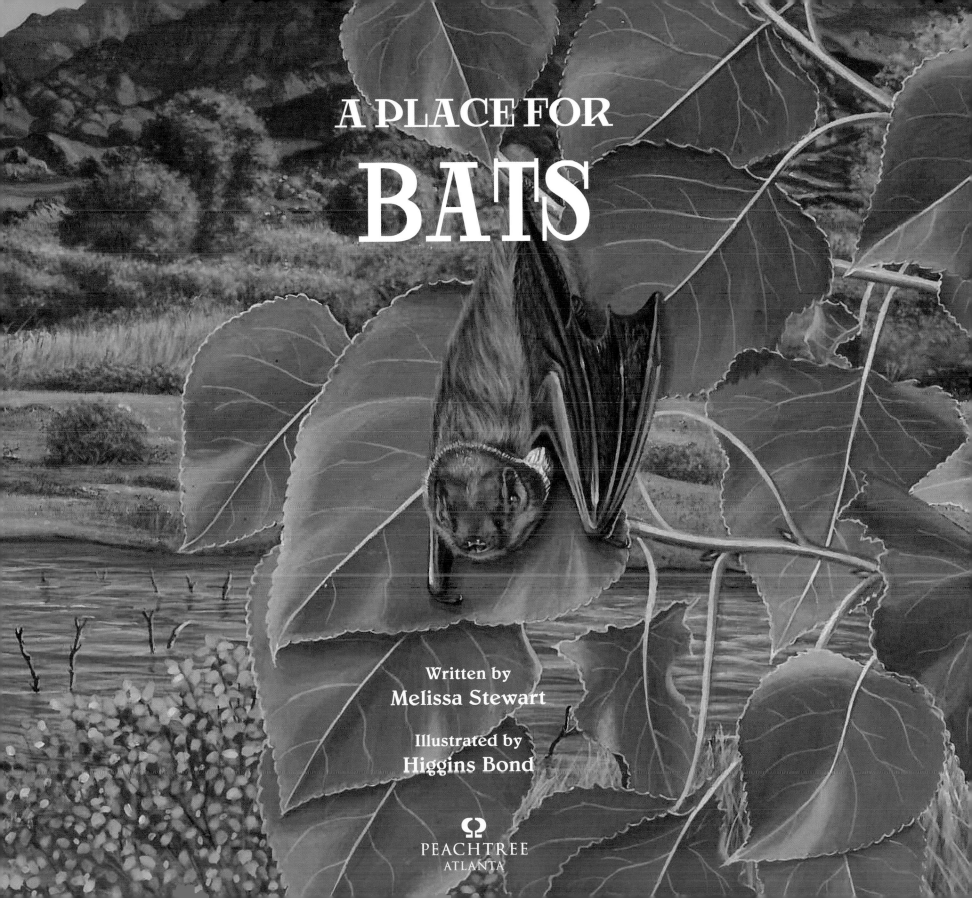

# A PLACE FOR
# BATS

Written by
**Melissa Stewart**

Illustrated by
**Higgins Bond**

PEACHTREE
ATLANTA

Bats make our world a better place. But sometimes people do things that make it hard for them to live and grow.

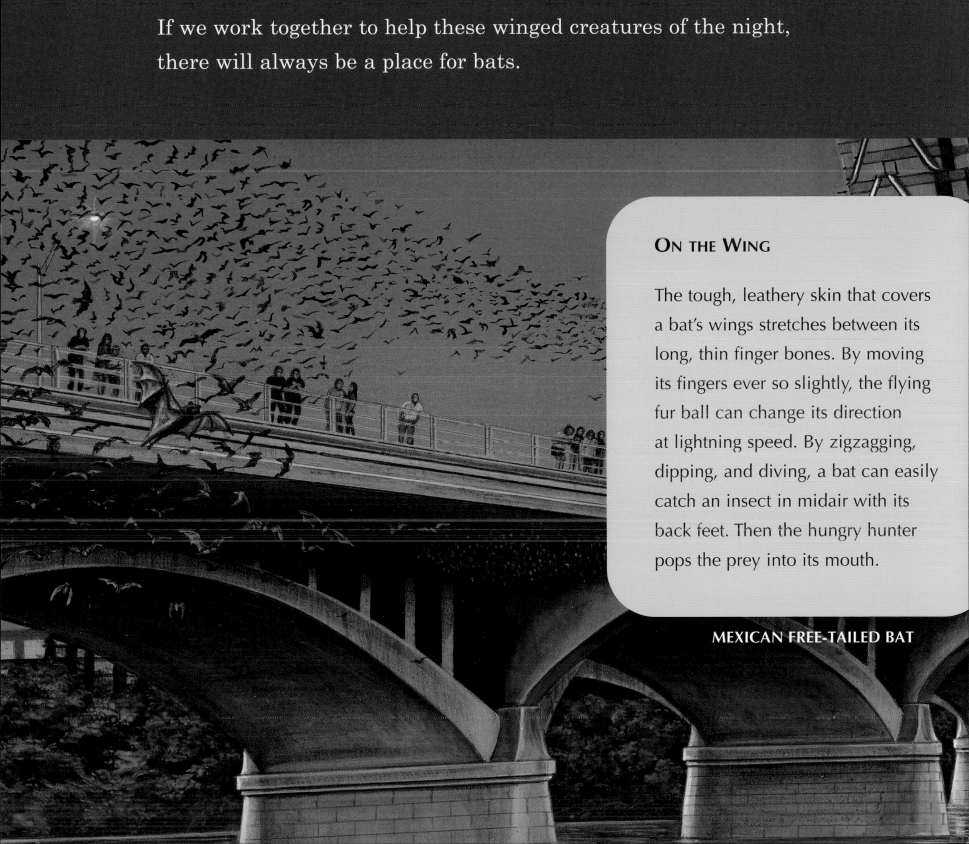

If we work together to help these winged creatures of the night, there will always be a place for bats.

### ON THE WING

The tough, leathery skin that covers a bat's wings stretches between its long, thin finger bones. By moving its fingers ever so slightly, the flying fur ball can change its direction at lightning speed. By zigzagging, dipping, and diving, a bat can easily catch an insect in midair with its back feet. Then the hungry hunter pops the prey into its mouth.

MEXICAN FREE-TAILED BAT

For bats to survive, they need to stay safe and healthy. Many bats are killed by people who think bats are dangerous.

## INDIANA BAT

In the 1800s, millions of Indiana bats spent the winter in caves in Kentucky, Missouri, and Indiana. People snuck into some of the caves and killed the bats with clubs. Sometimes they set fires so the bats would burn. By the 1960s, almost all the bats were gone. Today, groups like Bat Conservation International are letting people know that bats are an important part of our world. Hopefully, educating people will help save Indiana bats.

But bats can't hurt us, and they devour pesky insects all night long.
When people learn the truth about these little nighttime flyers,
bats can live and grow.

Some bats die when they fly too close to the wind turbines people use to make electricity.

## HOARY BAT

In 2008, scientists discovered that when a hoary bat flies through the low-pressure area around a wind turbine's blades, the air inside its lungs suddenly expands. Blood vessels around the lungs burst, and the bat dies. Once scientists understood the problem, they figured out how to solve it. Bats are most active on calm nights, when wind turbines don't produce much power. If power companies turn off their turbines when the wind isn't blowing, they can save hoary bats and still produce plenty of electricity.

When people turn off wind turbines on calm nights, bats can live and grow.

A bat can drown if it gets trapped in a watering trough for thirsty cattle or horses.

When ranch owners add escape ramps to their watering troughs, bats can live and grow.

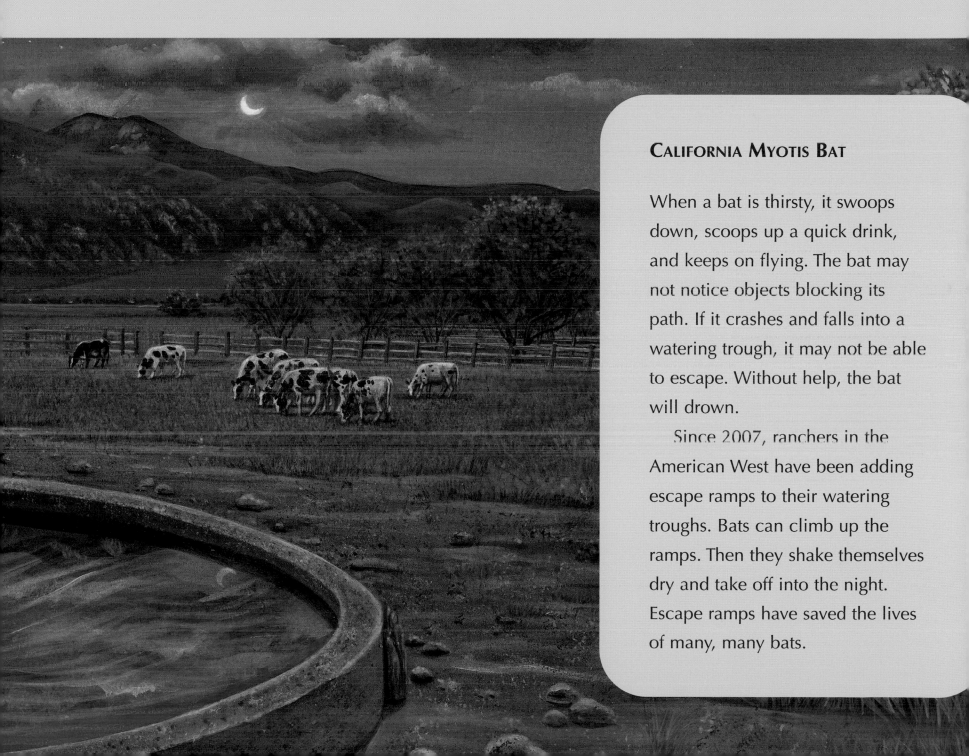

### CALIFORNIA MYOTIS BAT

When a bat is thirsty, it swoops down, scoops up a quick drink, and keeps on flying. The bat may not notice objects blocking its path. If it crashes and falls into a watering trough, it may not be able to escape. Without help, the bat will drown.

Since 2007, ranchers in the American West have been adding escape ramps to their watering troughs. Bats can climb up the ramps. Then they shake themselves dry and take off into the night. Escape ramps have saved the lives of many, many bats.

Thousands of bats are dying of a terrible disease called white nose syndrome. Scientists think it is caused by a fungus that came from Europe.

When scientists discover a way to treat the disease, bats can live and grow.

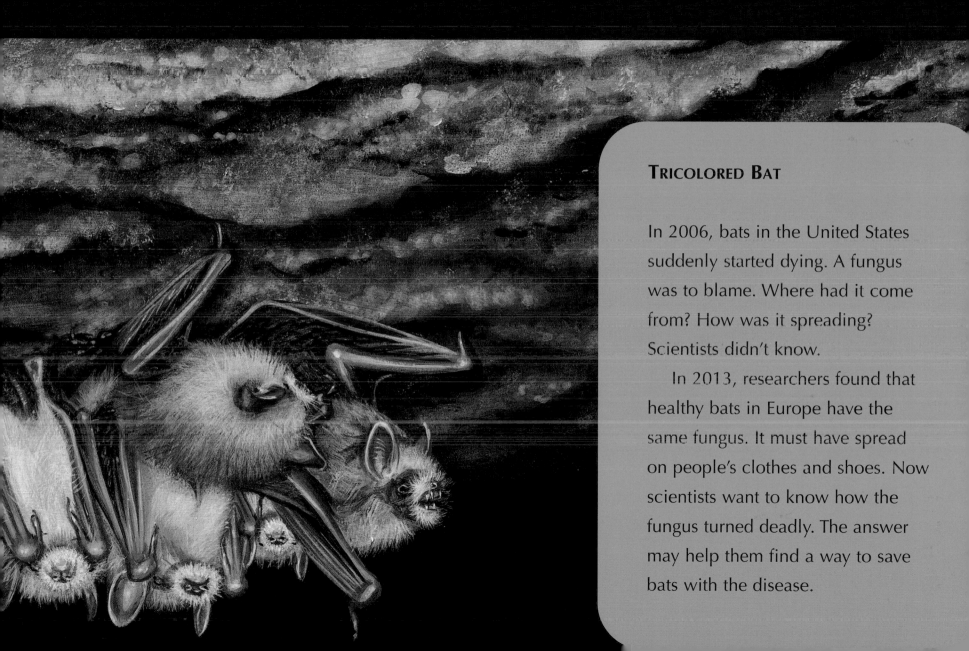

### TRICOLORED BAT

In 2006, bats in the United States suddenly started dying. A fungus was to blame. Where had it come from? How was it spreading? Scientists didn't know.

In 2013, researchers found that healthy bats in Europe have the same fungus. It must have spread on people's clothes and shoes. Now scientists want to know how the fungus turned deadly. The answer may help them find a way to save bats with the disease.

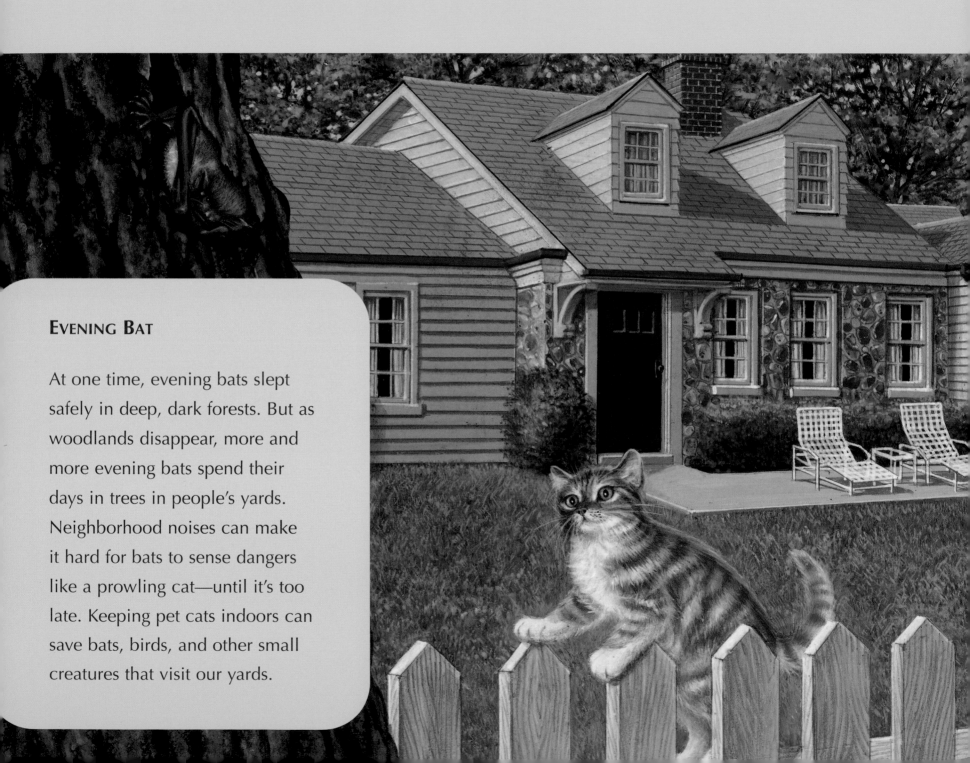

Some bats spend their days sleeping in trees in people's yards.
If a hungry housecat spots these bats, it will attack.

**EVENING BAT**

At one time, evening bats slept safely in deep, dark forests. But as woodlands disappear, more and more evening bats spend their days in trees in people's yards. Neighborhood noises can make it hard for bats to sense dangers like a prowling cat—until it's too late. Keeping pet cats indoors can save bats, birds, and other small creatures that visit our yards.

When people keep their pet cats indoors, bats can live and grow.

Bats also need safe places to raise their young. Some bat pups grow up inside caves.

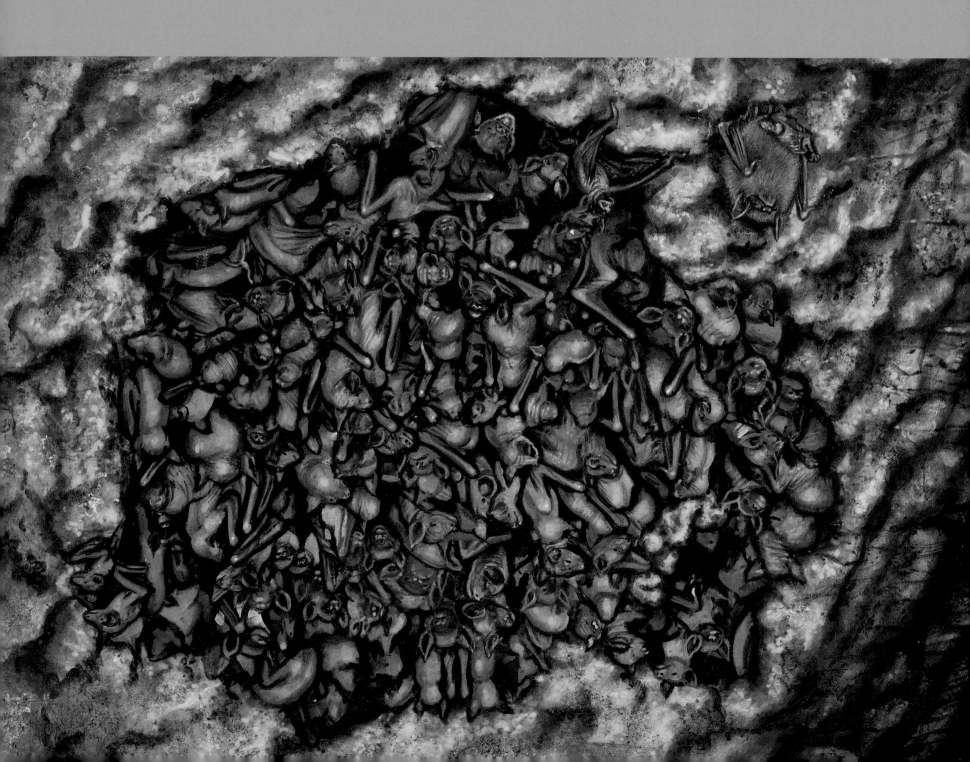

When workers build gates to keep out curious explorers,
bats can live and grow.

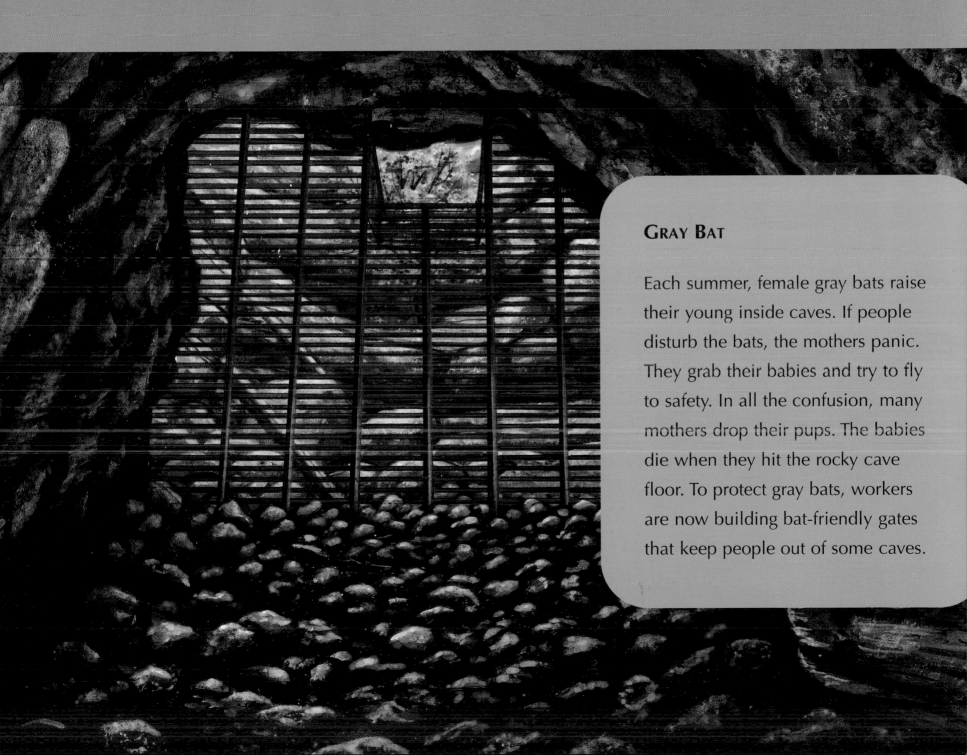

### GRAY BAT

Each summer, female gray bats raise
their young inside caves. If people
disturb the bats, the mothers panic.
They grab their babies and try to fly
to safety. In all the confusion, many
mothers drop their pups. The babies
die when they hit the rocky cave
floor. To protect gray bats, workers
are now building bat-friendly gates
that keep people out of some caves.

## Little Brown Bat

In the past, little brown bats raised their young under the peeling bark of dead trees. But then people began cutting down the dead trees on their land. Luckily, some people noticed the problem and started building bat boxes. Today you can see these boxes in backyards and wooded areas all over North America.

When people build bat boxes that are the right size and shape,
bats can live and grow.

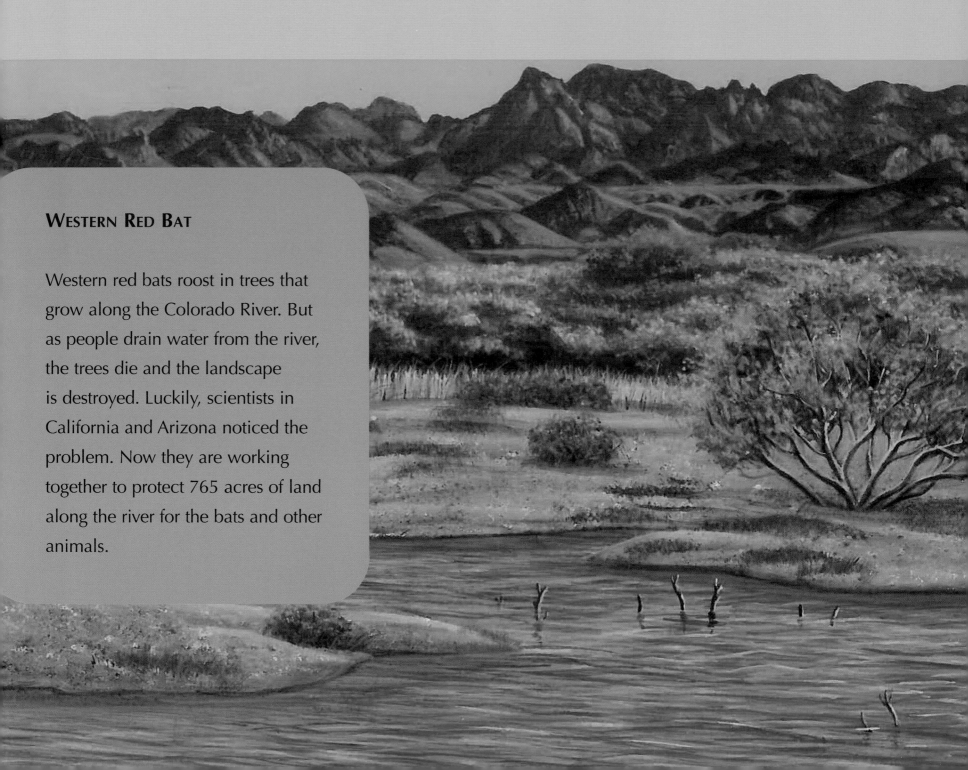

Bats have trouble surviving when their home habitats are destroyed. Some bats can only live in open woodlands with rivers or streams nearby.

## WESTERN RED BAT

Western red bats roost in trees that grow along the Colorado River. But as people drain water from the river, the trees die and the landscape is destroyed. Luckily, scientists in California and Arizona noticed the problem. Now they are working together to protect 765 acres of land along the river for the bats and other animals.

When people set aside some of these natural areas, bats can live and grow.

Other bats can only survive in thick forests with lots of large, old trees.

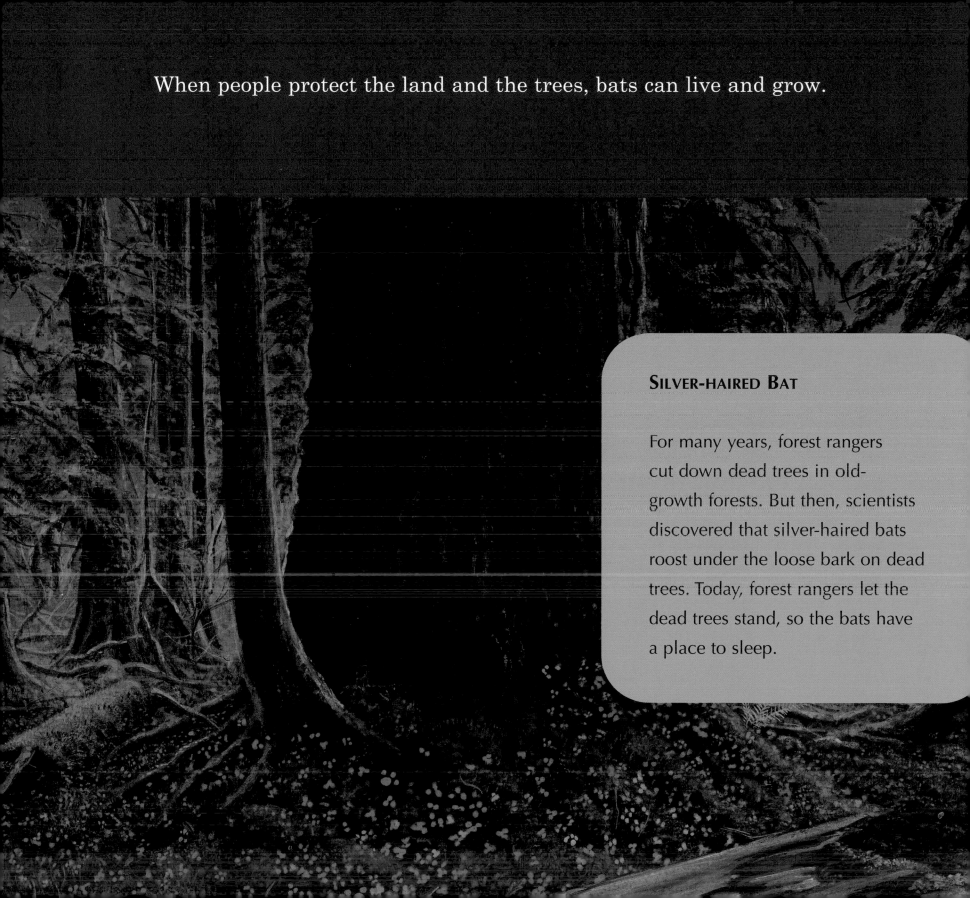

When people protect the land and the trees, bats can live and grow.

### SILVER-HAIRED BAT

For many years, forest rangers cut down dead trees in old-growth forests. But then, scientists discovered that silver-haired bats roost under the loose bark on dead trees. Today, forest rangers let the dead trees stand, so the bats have a place to sleep.

Some bats spend their days sleeping in palm trees. They stay safe from enemies by hiding under dead, leaf-like fronds.

When people leave the old, drooping fronds on the trees in their yards, bats can live and grow.

### NORTHERN YELLOW BAT

Many people do not like the way dead, brown fronds look hanging from palm trees. They trim the fronds so the trees will look neat and tidy. But recently, people in South Texas have realized that northern yellow bats roost under the fronds. So now some area residents are leaving dead fronds on their trees so the bats have a safe place to sleep.

Thousands of bats can die when people block the openings of old, abandoned mines.

## Big Brown Bat

Open mine shafts can be dangerous, so landowners often fill them in. But if there are bats inside, they will be buried alive. Just before Millie Hill Mine in Iron Mountain, Michigan, was supposed to be closed, scientists found millions of big brown bats inside. Instead of blocking the shaft, workers built a steel cage around the opening. Now bats can easily fly in and out, but no one will fall into the mine.

When people check old mines before filling them with rocks and dirt,
bats can live and grow.

When too many bats die, other living things may also have trouble surviving.

## PLANTS NEED BATS

In warm parts of the world, some bats sip sugary nectar from flowers. As they drink, the bats spread pollen from one flower to another. The plants use material in the pollen to make fruit with new seeds inside.

Other bats eat fruit. When the bats release their wastes, seeds land on the ground. If the soil is rich and moist, the seeds will grow into new plants. Bananas, peaches, avocados, dates, figs, and mangos all depend on bats to spread their pollen and to carry their seeds to new places.

That's why it's so important to protect bats and the places where they live.

### OTHER ANIMALS NEED BATS

Bats are an important part of the food chain. Hungry snakes, raccoons, opossums, skunks, and weasels sometimes prey on bats sleeping in trees. Hawks and owls can catch bats as they fly through the air. If too many bats disappear, their predators will have to work harder to find food.

LESSER LONG-NOSED BAT

**B**ats have lived on Earth for more than 50 million years.

## HOW BATS HELP US

Bats help us survive. By eating insects, bats protect the plants growing in farmers' fields. Each night, the Mexican free-tailed bats living in one cave in Texas devour 400,000 pounds of crop-eating insects. Bats also eat mosquitoes and other insects that can make us sick. A little brown bat can catch 1,000 mosquitoes in just one hour.

Sometimes people do things that can harm bats. But there are many ways you can help these special creatures live far into the future.

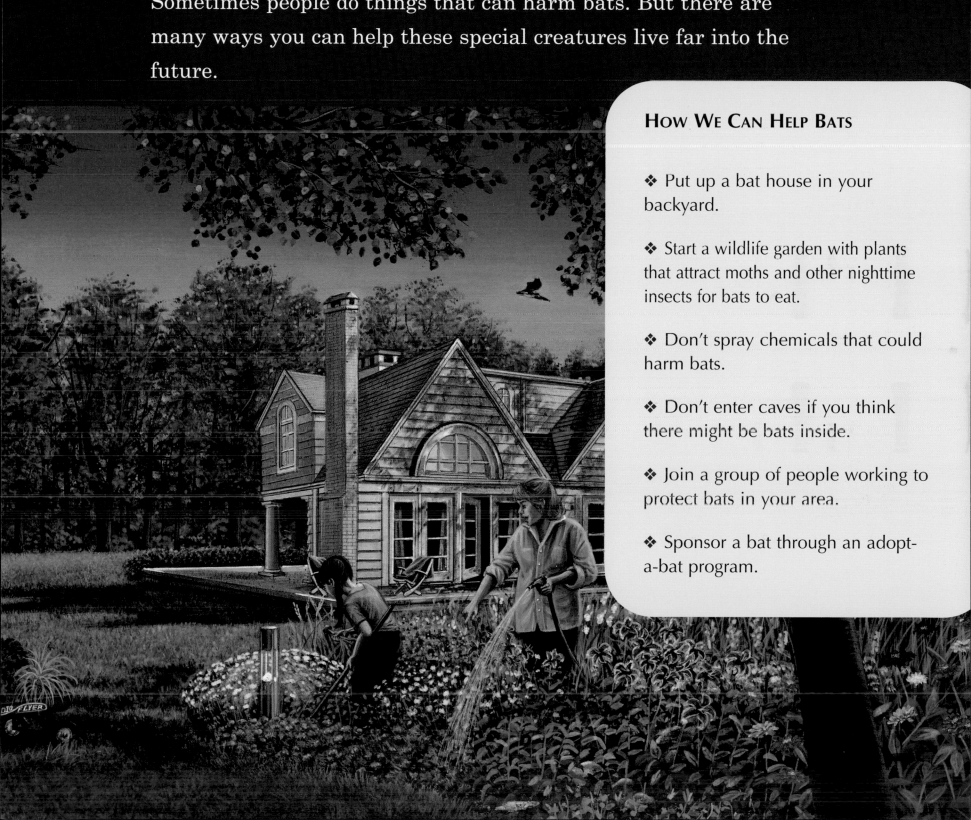

## How We Can Help Bats

❖ Put up a bat house in your backyard.

❖ Start a wildlife garden with plants that attract moths and other nighttime insects for bats to eat.

❖ Don't spray chemicals that could harm bats.

❖ Don't enter caves if you think there might be bats inside.

❖ Join a group of people working to protect bats in your area.

❖ Sponsor a bat through an adopt-a-bat program.

## Bat Facts

* No one knows exactly how many kinds of bats live on Earth. So far, scientists have discovered more than 1,200 different species. Forty-five kinds of bats live in North America.
* Almost all of the bats in North America and 70 percent of bats worldwide eat insects. But some bats eat fruit, nectar, fish, frogs, lizards, and birds.

* The Kitti's hog-nosed bat is the smallest bat on Earth. It's about the size of a bumblebee. The flying fox is the world's largest bat. Its wings can stretch five feet.
* Bats are the only mammals that can fly. The big brown bat is the world's fastest bat. It can cruise through the air at forty miles per hour.
* Blood-sucking vampire bats in Central and South America usually feed on chickens, turkeys, ducks, and geese. Sometimes they drink blood from pigs, cattle, and horses.

### Selected Bibliography

Di Silvestro, Roger. "Drinking on the Fly: The Unique Habits of Thirsty Bats Are Putting the Animals at Risk throughout the Arid West, but a Simple Solution May Solve this Problem." *National Wildlife,* June 1, 2007, pp. 31–37.

Fenton, M. Brock and Nancy B. Simmons. *Bats: A World of Science and Mystery.* Chicago, IL: Chicago University Press, 2015.

"Gray Bat Fact Sheet," U.S. Fish & Wildlife Services. Available online at *http://www.fws.gov/midwest/Endangered/mammals/grbat_fc.html*

Toops, Connie. "Going to Bat for Bats." *National Parks.* Jan-Feb 2001: pp. 28–31.

Tuttle, Merlin D. *America's Neighborhood Bats.* Austin, TX: University of Texas Press, 2005.

Tuttle, Merlin D. *The Secret Lives of Bats.* Boston, MA: Houghton Mifflin, 2015.

Warnecke, L., J. M. Turner, T. K. Bollinger, J. M. Lorch, V. Misra, P. M. Cryan, G. Wibbelt, D. S. Blehert, and C. K. R. Willis. "Inoculation of bats with European *Geomyces destructans* supports the novel pathogen hypothesis for the origin of white-nose syndrome." *Proceedings of the National Academy of Sciences of the United States of America.* May 1, 2012, pp. 6999–7003.

"Western Red Bat," Lower Colorado River Multi-Species Conservation Program.

### Recommended for Young Readers

Bat Conservation International. *http://www.batcon.org/*

Carney, Elizabeth. *Bats.* Washington, DC: National Geographic Society, 2010.

Davies, Nicola. *Bat Loves the Night.* Cambridge, MA: Candlewick, 2004.

Defenders of Wildlife: Bats.
   *http://www.defenders.org/wildlife_and_habitat/wildlife/bats.php#*

Markle, Sandra. *Little Lost Bat.* Watertown, MA: Charlesbridge, 2009.

Williams, Kim, Rob Mies, and Donald and Lillian Stokes. *Stokes Beginner's Guide to Bats.* New York: Little, Brown & Company, 2002.

### Acknowledgments

The Smithsonian National Museum of Natural History provided range maps and habitat data for most of the bats discussed in this book.